Dear Reader

My grandfather loved "westerns" and kept a drawer full of paperback "western" novels in his study. I used to read them, and I remember the action, settings and characters in those books aways seemed colourful and larger than life. Years later, I wanted to write my own "western" – and here it is!

Stella Santa Cruz
Author

The United States

1. Utah
2. Colorado
3. Kansas
4. Missouri

1 A True Story?

With a satisfied press of the "enter" button, the old man finished his work at the computer and relaxed in his comfortable leather chair.

A surreptitious glance at his wristwatch confirmed that it was late and he'd been working at home for more hours than he'd expected. "I spend far too much time in this office," he declared. But, ever since he'd been elected, he'd accepted that being a United States Congressman meant he could never expect to keep regular hours. The incessant demands of having an important role in government made sure of that.

The heavy oak door to the congressman's home office creaked open and a pair of hopeful eyes peered up at him.

"Grandad, it's almost bedtime," said his grandson. "Can you tell me a story?"

"Sure," smiled the old man. He swung the young boy up on his knee. "What kind of story would you like to hear?"

The Great Golden Nugget of Utah

Written by Stella Santa Cruz
Illustrated by Scott Fraser

Contents

Meet the Characters

Jake

An army deserter.

Washington

A runaway slave.

Ulysses

Jake's horse (pronounced "*you-le-sees*").

Toovuts

A native American chief.

"Just make one up," replied the boy. "Mum says you're good at making up stories. It's your job."

The old man chuckled. "I guess it is an occupational hazard," he replied. "Well, I ..." The man glanced around his office for inspiration. And then his eyes fell upon a small plaque that proudly framed his family's coat of arms.

The congressman pursed his lips thoughtfully and glanced down at his grandson. It was probably time to tell him the story that he'd been saving for the right moment – the story that had been passed down to him from his grandfather.

"How about a story called *The Great Golden Nugget of Utah*?" suggested the old man.

The boy's eyes widened. "Wow," he said. "That sounds exciting. Is it a true story?"

"Well," said his grandfather, clearing his throat. "Why don't I just tell the story, and let's see if you can guess."

2 A Man and His Horse

When Jake threw the bone-dry twigs he'd collected onto the fire, flames transformed them into embers the colour of fantastic scarlet rubies and tangerine topaz.

Flickering shadows distorted the outline of his horse, Ulysses, into a shimmering steed that trembled across the sandstone behind his flank. A spire of smoke curled lazily into the calm night air.

Above the lone man and horse, a band of glittering stars stretched from horizon to horizon, as if someone had used a giant celestial paintbrush to splash a swathe of diamonds across the heavens.

The enormous night seemed to swallow every sound, except for the occasional click of iron shoe upon stone, as Ulysses shifted his weight from one hoof to another – and the occasional click of steel upon steel, as Jake checked his Smith and Wesson revolver.

Since Jake had deserted from the rebel Confederate army fighting a bitter civil war against Union soldiers from the north, his trustworthy revolver had become

one of only two friends he could depend upon. The other was Ulysses, who asked only for a handful of oats in return for carrying Jake further and further away from the troubled southern battlefields.

Together, they had ridden out of the new state of Missouri, westwards across the lawless territory of Kansas. Slowly, as the weeks transformed themselves into months, they moved through a wilderness area whose Spanish name reflected its rocks and soils – colorado or "red-coloured". Finally, the horse and its rider had made it into Utah, the wild territory named after the Native American tribe who lived there. Settlers who ventured this far found the uncompromising territory and its inhabitants tough – as the deserted, half-burned farmhouse he'd passed earlier in the day had testified.

"Ulysses, my friend," said Jake, as he lay down on the unforgiving sandstone and gazed up at the stars. "There's a mighty fine show twinkling up there for us tonight."

Ulysses whinnied gently, the firelight glinting in his tired brown eyes.

"There's just you and me, the rocks and the sky, and no one else for a hundred miles," said Jake contentedly. "I'm guessing this'll be the closest we ever get to being free."

Jake knew the unfortunate fate that awaited deserters who were captured. This far west, most people were a law unto themselves, and it was difficult to tell whether they were pro-Union or pro-Confederate. Jake took the sensible approach, which was that regardless of which side they supported, everybody was pro-reward. The twenty silver dollars placed on the capture of a deserter was enough to sway anyone's opinions.

Consequently, he and Ulysses avoided the few towns and outposts along their slow, dusty route westwards, preferring the splendid, peaceful isolation of the prairies and the desert. There, no one would ask awkward questions. No one would wonder aloud about the lone rider and his horse. No one would pay a second thought to what direction they were heading, or what circumstances they were leaving behind.

A glowing ember exploded with a fierce "crack" and, for a second, all of Jake's senses were instantly alert. His right hand shot instinctively towards the bone handle of the Smith and Wesson revolver on his belt. A shower of orange sparks rose from the campfire, and Jake flicked his eyes across at Ulysses. A wary horse was the best alarm that Jake could wish for – but Ulysses's ears and tail remained motionless, and he just shuffled his hooves restlessly.

Jake relaxed and he loosened his grip on the revolver. Tonight, there was no danger. He lay his head upon the brim of his hat. Through the dusty felt, the warmth of the sandstone was comforting, and Jake went back to counting glittering diamonds in the sky.

3 A Thunderous Shock

That evening, Jake slept fitfully, drifting in and out of consciousness as the restless hours wore on.

His bones were used to sleeping on a hard rock bed, night after night, but in the silence of the darkness, his mind came alive with the roar of cannon fire, the fearsome rush of hand-to-hand fighting and the gruesome sights of the battles he was trying to leave behind.

Suddenly, a thunderous boom split the night sky and Jake bolted upright, his heart thumping, his right hand desperately feeling for the steely reassurance of his revolver's trigger. Ulysses was tossing his head wildly. He rose on his powerful hind legs, kicking his forelegs in alarm.

Instantly awake, Jake dropped flat on his stomach and looked around wildly.

At that very second, a gigantic red gash seared above them, tearing the dark sky apart like a terrible wound.

Jake's head was spinning. What was going on? What was this terrifying apparition?

Before he could unscramble his thoughts, another gigantic boom crashed through the air, sending thundering shock waves through the air, the rocks and Jake's sprawled body.

All he could think of were huge cannons, unleashing a deadly assault all around him. But why? He was only a lone deserter. Surely, the Confederate army wouldn't have risked horses and men hauling heavy cannons and ammunition through one dangerous state and two wild territories just for him?

He pressed his face into the sandstone, covered his head with his forearms, and waited for the next bombardment.

It never came.

Jake's heart was pounding. He sensed that if he was being attacked, this was the most dangerous moment of all. He had seen enough battles to know that, as soon as the cannon fire ceased, enemy troops would advance to quickly take advantage of their shocked foe.

Keeping flat to the ground, he rolled himself over and over, until he reached a small hollow in the natural wall of sandstone that sheltered his campsite. He quickly checked over the edge of the wall. Nothing. He strained his ears, listening for the slightest sound of approaching metal on metal, boots upon rock. Again, nothing.

He pressed his spine into the curve of the hollow, gritted his teeth and aimed his revolver out into the menacing darkness. He waited. And waited.

In the vastness of the desert, the sounds of the night seemed magnified a hundred-fold. Suddenly, there it was! A metallic sound!

Every hair on Jake's neck and arms stood on end. A dark shadow loomed out of the inky blackness. Jake swirled around, simultaneously aiming his weapon and pulling back the hammer on his revolver. And then ...

The shadow gave a low whinny and took another step closer. Horseshoe met rock. A tail swished in the desert air.

"Ulysses!" cried Jake, relief flooding over him as the tension vanished. "Come here, boy."

Ulysses obediently trotted over to Jake, giving him a gentle nuzzle with his nose.

"Are you OK, Ulysses?" murmured Jake. He noticed that Ulysses no longer seemed nervous or agitated. That meant that the danger, whatever it was, was no longer nearby.

Nevertheless, Jake was determined to remain cautious. He grabbed his hat and hurriedly kicked sand over the last of the campfire's embers, extinguishing the red glow that might be spotted by an eagle-eyed enemy soldier.

Quietly and swiftly, Jake packed up his few possessions, pulled his hat low over his eyes and led Ulysses away from the campsite. He'd noticed a deep, bone-dry creek bed the evening before, heading southwards from the deserted, burnt-out farmhouse. He decided he was going to head for the creek bed. Its rocky banks were at least half the height of a man standing in his boots, and that would provide at least some cover if the attack started again.

Ten minutes passed, and then fifteen. Jake was confident they'd be close to the dry creek by now.

Finally, he saw a dark shadow snaking its way across the landscape ahead and he knew they'd made it to safety.

Coaxing Ulysses along, Jake knew he'd have to jump into the deep creek bed first. It was dark, and no horse, not even the ever-faithful Ulysses, would be willing to jump anywhere where it couldn't see the ground beneath itself. The horse seemed nervous, tossing its head and twitching its ears as they reached the edge of the dark creek.

"Don't worry, boy," said Jake soothingly. "I'll go first. It's only waist high. You'll get down easily."

Jake jumped into the darkness, and landed easily, knees bent. The dry creek bed was solid enough for Ulysses not to stumble or twist a ligament when he jumped. Jake was about to rise up and persuade Ulysses to join him when he got the second shock of the night.

Two unblinking eyes were staring back at him from a small hollow beneath the creek bank. And between those eyes, held straight out towards Jake, was the menacing barrel of another Smith and Wesson. Except this time, Smith and Wesson were not his friends.

"Hands up!" growled a threatening voice.

4 Friend or Foe?

The fingers on Jake's right hand twitched as they hovered above his holster. He was quick on the draw – but he knew he wasn't *that* quick.

Reluctantly, he slowly raised his hands, straining his eyes to see whether the shadowy figure crouched against the creek bed was wearing a Union or Confederate uniform.

"Take it easy, friend," he murmured in a calm voice that belied the adrenalin pumping through his veins like a bolt of frozen lightning. Still he couldn't see whether his captor wore the grey uniform of a friend or the dark blue uniform of a foe.

Ulysses, who remained standing on the edge of the creek bed, suddenly let out a furious snort and tossed his head angrily. He stamped his front hoof noisily, and Jake seized his chance.

In the split second that Ulysses distracted his captor, Jake dropped to the bed of the dark creek and rolled over. Simultaneously, his hand found the comforting wooden and ivory grip of his own revolver.

With his other hand, he grabbed a handful of loose stones from the creek bed and hurled them at his adversary's face.

He rolled again and his shoulder crashed into the other bank of the creek, opposite the shadowy figure. Disoriented by the sudden events, the mysterious figure lost sight of Jake, and instantly the roles were reversed.

"Now you put *your* hands up," growled Jake. Hidden in the darkness, Smith and Wesson had become his best friends again, and the shadow opposite him knew it. The figure's bravado evaporated and his revolver clattered to the ground, and he raised his trembling hands in surrender.

"Now stand up where I can see you," instructed Jake. Despite the order, the figure appeared to stay crouching beneath the top of the creek bank.

"I said stand up," growled Jake menacingly.

"I am standing up," insisted the other voice.

Jake peered through the darkness at the figure and realised with a shock that he wasn't wearing a Union or a Confederate uniform. He was barefoot and wearing torn and ragged clothes. And he was standing up. The figure that had confronted him couldn't have been more than eleven years old.

“What on earth ...?” gasped Jake, his voice trailing off in astonishment. He lowered his weapon and stared at the boy in front of him. “Who are you? And what are you doing here?”

“My name is Washington,” replied the boy defiantly, puffing out his chest. “And I am a freeman.”

Jake pushed his hat back on his forehead and looked at the boy.

“A freeman,” he said, raising one eyebrow quizzically. “Is that so?”

“Yes, sir,” replied Washington, matter-of-factly.

“Well, I’m pleased to meet you, Washington. I don’t think we’ve been introduced properly. My name’s Jake. And that there’s Ulysses.”

Jake knew exactly what a freeman was. That was mostly what the war he was escaping from was about. He held out his hand, and Washington nervously shook it.

“I guess I’m kind of a freeman, too,” added Jake.

Jake and Washington eyed one another, each pondering this information and deciding if they could trust the other. Both being freemen meant they had some things in common.

Both of them had a long way to go before they were really free. Both of them had a considerable reward on their heads. And both of them were on the run – Jake from the Confederate army and Washington from the southern slave owners.

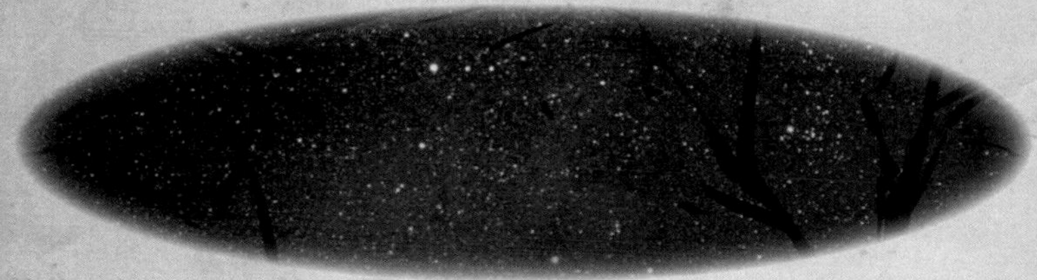

"I guess you got spooked by the same thing as I did," said Jake. "I thought there were cannons and all sorts of things being let loose upon me."

Washington nodded. "Yes, sir. Whatever it was, it wasn't cannons. I've been hiding out in that old abandoned farmhouse for days. There's no food – but there's a tiny freshwater spring you can drink from. No one's been by, not even riding in the distance."

Jake rested against the bank of the creek. "I gave up calling people 'sir' one state and two territories ago," he said. "I reckon I wouldn't be offended if you gave it up, too."

"Yes, sir," grinned Washington. "I mean, Jake, sir."

Jake got to his feet and gave a low whistle. Ulysses raised his head from a clump of wiry grass he'd been investigating and trotted obediently towards the creek.

Jake climbed up the stony creek bank and unstrapped one of Ulysses's saddlebags. He drew out an old blanket and tossed it towards Washington. Then he untied a rough canvas bedroll from behind the saddle, and clambered back down into the dry creek bed.

"I reckon we've had plenty of excitement for one night," he said. "I'm getting some shut-eye."

He narrowed his eyes and looked at Washington. "Ulysses don't take kindly to folks who engage in horse rustling," he warned. "So I hope you haven't got any silly ideas about stealing my horse and running off in the middle of the night."

"No, sir," replied Washington. "I mean, no. Sir."

"Darn it," thought Jake to himself. "I reckon it's going to take some time to fix that bad habit."

5 The Shooting Star

"Somehow," thought Jake, "bones and rocks don't ever seem to find themselves a place where they're both happy."

He yawned and stretched his aching limbs. His bruised shoulder hurt where he'd rolled violently into the creek bank last night, and he rubbed it ruefully.

The sun was just breaking over the horizon, and the dry, deserted landscape was flooded with the scarlet and tangerine shades of a Utah dawn.

Jake glanced over at the huddled figure of Washington, still fast asleep beneath his borrowed blanket. He heard Ulysses, gently puffing his nostrils close by, and he rose to his feet.

"I hear you, my friend," said Jake. "You never forget to remind me about that handful of oats you like for breakfast."

He dusted off his shirt, found his hat and clambered up the bank. He wandered over to the sandstone outcrop where Ulysses was patiently waiting. Jake was about to untie the sack of oats from his saddle when he glanced at the red landscape illuminated by the sun's rays beyond his horse.

"Well, I'll be ..." he said. "Would you look at that?"

Jake stared at the landscape in awe until a sound behind him caught his attention. He turned and saw Washington staggering wearily towards the small rise where he and Ulysses stood.

"Morning, sir," yawned Washington. "I mean, morning ..."

The boy rubbed the last of the sleep out of his eyes and looked up at Jake and Ulysses. Then his eyes opened wide and he stared in the same direction as Jake.

"I guess we've now solved the mystery of those midnight cannons," observed Jake.

For what seemed like ages, Jake, Washington and Ulysses stayed motionless on the outcrop. The only movement came from their slowly lengthening shadows, growing gradually behind them as the sun climbed over the amazing panorama of devastation in front of them.

"Sleeping out, I've seen plenty of shooting stars," whistled Jake. "And I've heard that, now and again, some of them tumble all the way down to Earth. But I've never seen anything like that."

To the east, the morning light revealed a giant elliptical crater where the night before there had been only weathered sandstone ridges and columns. Everything had been flattened by the impact, except for a curving, stony ridge of earth and rock that had been pushed up by the unimaginable force of the meteorite crashing into the desert.

There was nothing left of the meteorite, which had been instantly blasted into a million fragments by the impact. But the evidence of its fiery arrival in the Utah desert would be plain to see for many years.

"Can we go and see if we can find a piece of shooting star?" asked Washington eagerly. "I reckon if we carried a piece of shooting star with us, it would be certain to bring us nothing but good luck."

"We already had good luck, with it choosing not to come landing on top of us," said Jake. But he was curious too, and eventually he nodded at Washington. "I guess there's no harm in taking a look for some more good luck."

Jake and Washington gathered their few possessions, and Jake saddled up Ulysses ready for the ride down to the crater. He swung himself up into the saddle, and held a hand out to Washington.

Washington gave him a puzzled look.

"You coming up or what?" invited Jake impatiently.

"You mean I can ride on Ulysses?" said Washington. Horses were for slave owners and soldiers and cowboys. He'd never ridden one.

Jake looked around. "I don't see no other horses," he replied. "You coming up or what?"

"Yes, SIR!" shouted Washington in excitement. Jake sighed and figured he'd let that one go.

Wedged together in the saddle, Jake and Washington allowed Ulysses to pick his way eastwards. Jake pulled his hat low to keep the morning sun out of his eyes. In front of him, Washington proudly gripped the reins with one hand, the other cupped against his forehead.

Jake knew he could let Ulysses find his own way, and Washington seemed to be excited to just hold the reins. Jake was satisfied to contemplate the scene in front of them and to keep a wary eye out for any unwelcome strangers in the distance. They might be freemen, but only as long as there was no one else around to disturb their freedom with prying questions.

After about quarter of an hour in the hot sun, Ulysses' hooves started to crunch on the glassy fragments that lay in broad swathes near the crater's edge.

"Stop here," said Jake. Washington looked around in bewilderment, not knowing what to do. "Give Ulysses a gentle tug on the reins," explained Jake. "He'll know what that means."

Washington gave a sharp tug on the reins. Ulysses came to a halt with a snort, turning his head towards Washington as if to say, "Gently. I think my master said 'gently'."

Jake climbed down and helped Washington clamber off the horse.

"I don't want any of these shards to get lodged in a hoof," he said, grinding a fragment of glass under his heel. "A lame horse is all we need, out here in the desert."

He unlooped the reins and secured one end under a large rock.

"Don't go anywhere, boy," he said to Ulysses, who blinked in acknowledgment.

Jake and Washington left the horse and picked their way across the mounds of pebbles, earth and glass fragments towards the rim of the crater.

Washington spied a smooth tear-shaped fragment of glass that looked like a molten drop of ebony that had solidified in mid-air.

"That's got to be a piece of shooting star," he said excitedly, putting the glass in his pocket. "Ouch!" Too late, he noticed the razor sharp edge of the teardrop.

"Reckon you might be right," nodded Jake. Washington ran off to climb the rim of the crater.

Jake looked around at the pummelled earth, covered with fragments of glass glinting in the sun. There was nothing of any value here, he decided. At least the boy had his piece of shooting star, and he hoped that would keep him quiet for the rest of the day.

He turned around and was about to crunch his way back towards Ulysses when his eye caught a flash of sunlight reflecting off something else. But it wasn't black like the shattered glass lying everywhere. It had a gleam that was more the colour of calm water reflecting a warm evening sun.

"I'm just going to see what that is," he called, with his back to Washington. There was no reply. At least that piece of shooting star is keeping him quiet, he thought. He walked over to where the gleaming object lay, and bent down for a closer look. He brushed the dust off the object. Then he scraped the earth from its edges. Then he blinked in astonishment and disbelief.

"Well, I'll be ..." breathed Jake, as it slowly dawned on him what the gnarled, gleaming object was. It was a solid lump of gold, the size of a grapefruit, embedded in the earth. He shot upright and whirled around to call Washington over.

Suddenly, he was struck speechless.

Washington, a terrified look in his eyes, had a heavily muscled arm locked around his neck. Behind the wriggling boy stood a towering Ute warrior brandishing a tomahawk.

Jake's heart sank. He knew the Ute people from this region were fierce fighters, feared for skirmishing with not only the settlers but also the neighbouring Navajo and Apache people.

That was the last thought he had. He heard a whistling sound, like something heavy rushing through the air, and then everything went black.

6 A Dangerous Wolf

Jake groaned. His head felt like someone was using a blunt horseshoe nail to unpick a rope knot that had lodged itself deep within his skull.

He blinked and struggled to focus his blurry vision. He attempted to rub his eyes and discovered that he couldn't move his hands. Ropes, bound tightly around his wrists, bit painfully into his skin.

"Jake," came an urgent whisper. "Jake, are you alright?"

Jake blinked again and turned in the direction of the whisper. A wave of throbbing pain crashed through the back of his head and splashed around behind his eyes, the aching foam obscuring his vision.

Slowly, the throbbing subsided and the image of Washington's face came into focus. After a few painful seconds, the face grew a neck, body and limbs and Jake saw that he, too, was tied to a post. Behind Washington, Jake could see a scattered collection of Ute teepees, with horses tethered nearby. He was relieved to see Ulysses was amongst the horses. At least he wasn't abandoned, wandering the rugged sandstone landscape in search of food or water.

"Never better," replied Jake, gritting his teeth. At least Washington had learnt to drop the "sir".

The hide flap covering the entrance of one of the teepees burst open and two men with braided hair strode purposefully towards Jake and Washington. Jake recognised one of them as the warrior who had been holding Washington. The other looked older and, from the impressive string of wolf fangs around his neck, Jake guessed he was the senior of the two. They stopped in front of Jake and the senior man spoke.

"I am Toovuts," he said, his forefinger tapping the fangs. Jake guessed that this was also the Ute name for a wolf. This man's name would reflect his personality, and wolves were dangerous and unpredictable.

"You are not welcome on our land. Your horse is the price you pay to trespass."

Jake remained silent. Tightly bound to a post in the earth, facing a man named after a vicious predator, was no place to argue.

"The greedy soldiers who march up and down, three days horse-ride to the west," continued Toovuts, nodding. "They will pay a good price for this yellow metal you have found. Because of this, you are lucky. We have sent a rider to tell them of this find. We will leave you here and when the soldiers arrive, you may still be alive."

"When they arrive ...?" said Jake. "What do you mean?"

"The soldiers must collect this thing. We will not touch it. It is like thunderwood. If any Ute handles thunderwood, the thunder beings will strike him down."

Thunderwood. Suddenly Jake realised that Toovuts was talking about wood from a tree that had been struck by lightning. Last night's meteorite had arrived with a thunderous boom and a gigantic red gash splitting the sky. No wonder these men weren't interested in touching the gold nugget.

Toovuts and the other warrior wheeled around and headed back to pack up their belongings and dismantle their teepee.

Washington looked at Jake.

"Three days?"

Jake grunted. He had spent enough time in the harsh wilderness areas to know that they could survive three days – as long as the Utes left them some water. He was more worried about Ulysses.

More Utes appeared from the teepees and loaded up their horses. Toovuts barked commands and the horses tethered around Ulysses stamped their hooves in excitement. One Ute untied the horses, one by one, in readiness for the ride ahead.

“Just keep quiet and let them go,” whispered Jake to Washington. “Once they’re out of sight, we’ll figure ...”

Jake was interrupted by a loud crack from where the horses were being readied. Men began shouting, and Jake saw Ulysses rising angrily onto his powerful hind legs. The Ute who had been untying the horses lay rolling on the ground, holding his ribs and moaning.

“Good on you, Ulysses,” smiled Jake grimly.

Toovuts shouted an order and a man with a rifle ran towards the horses. But the remainder of the alarmed horses had scattered and were galloping around the teepees. The man with the rifle aimed, but the dust thrown up by the hooves of the frightened horses meant he couldn’t get a clear shot at Ulysses.

In a whirlwind of dust, Jake’s horse galloped at a thundering pace towards the horizon.

“At least that makes one of us who is still a freeman,” growled Jake.

Toovuts shouted angrily and the rest of the men chased their horses until calm had been restored. Minutes later, the recaptured horses had been loaded with everything useful from the campsite. The Utes mounted the horses and waited for Toovuts to give the command.

With an angry look at Jake, Toovuts wheeled his horse around, and pressed his heels into the horse's flank. Like a tightly coiled spring suddenly released, the horse burst into a gallop. The other men formed a "V" behind Toovuts and within seconds, the Utes had gone.

As the relentless sound of hooves faded, Jake looked resignedly over at Washington. Securely tied to posts, in the hot Utah sun, he had a feeling this was going to be a miserable three days.

Washington slumped back against his post. The desert beyond them fell silent, and the unrelenting sun and the hopelessness of their plight beat down upon them.

"I guess they forgot to leave us the refreshing pitcher of lemonade," said Jake, trying to muster up all the humour he could manage.

7 The Golden Dilemma

Washington spent the next hour wriggling and twisting defiantly. The sturdy ropes binding his wrists rubbed his skin raw as he tried to squirm his body around.

"Save your energy," said Jake. "Those Utes know how to tie a knot. You'll never unpick it."

"No, I won't," grimaced Washington, as he stretched every muscle in his upper body. "But I have another idea."

His willed his fingers to reach lower, but his attempts were in vain. He moved his hips sideways until it felt like he was about to snap. And then, with a final groaning effort, his outstretched fingers found what they were searching for.

"Ouch," said Washington, straining. He shifted his hips back, and suddenly Jake could see what he was grasping.

The razor-sharp shard of glass. Their good luck piece of shooting star.

It took another half an hour of determined grunting to slice through each fibre of the ropes around his wrist, using the razor-sharp edge of the glass. But eventually Washington's efforts were rewarded and he broke free.

He struggled to stand upright on his aching legs, and he hobbled painfully across to Jake. Seconds later, they both stood, rubbing their wrists, freemen again.

"What now?" asked Washington.

"I don't know about you, but I'm getting me a handsome lump of gold," replied Jake. "That shooting star has already helped restore our freedom – but that golden nugget it uncovered is going to make sure we really are free men for the rest of our days."

An hour of exhausting trudging later, Jake and Washington reached the spot where they had discovered the great nugget the morning before. The Utes had left them with nothing, so at least they had nothing to weigh them down as they stumbled through the hot desert.

Jake spied the golden glint. The Utes were true to their word. They clearly wanted nothing to do with the object they associated with the cursed thunderwood. He fell excitedly to his knees and he and Washington dug around the nugget's edges with their bare hands. Finally, they prised the jagged lump of gold free.

Jake pulled off his shirt and made a sling for the heavy nugget. He lifted the sling over his shoulder and looked at Washington. "I need a drink," he said.

"Follow me," said Washington.

The abandoned farmhouse where Washington had been hiding out was about an hour's walk away. When they arrived, thirsty and hot, they made straight for the tiny spring that Washington had found a few days before. The water was warm and tasted faintly metallic, but they were both so thirsty they swallowed as much as they could.

Finally, his thirst satisfied, Jake sat back and looked around their surroundings. On the southern side, where the walls had been torched, the ruined farmhouse was open to the weather. A rusting anvil, some discarded blacksmith's tools, and some broken furniture lay scattered across the earthen floor.

"What now?" asked Washington, smearing a drop of water from his dusty face.

Jake pondered their options and concluded there weren't a great many of them. Together, they had nothing but the ragged clothes they wore and a lump of gold. Greedy soldiers, fired by the thought of the great nugget, would already be galloping their way. They, on the other hand, had no horse. They had no weapons. And Jake had no answer. He had no idea what to do next.

"Get some rest," he said. He hoped that an hour or two of shut-eye would somehow reveal an answer to their predicament. It wasn't much of a hope, he admitted to himself, but there appeared to be little alternative.

Something warm and wet, nuzzling into his ear, woke Jake with a start.

"What on earth ...?" He scrambled to his feet and whirled around. His right hand automatically dropped to his holster, but it was empty. The Utes had seen to that.

Jake's eyes widened when he saw what had woken him, and his face broke into a wide grin.

"Harrumph," puffed Ulysses reassuringly. He gently nudged Jake's face with his nose once more.

"Ulysses!" cried Jake. "Am I glad to see you!"

Washington, who had also been asleep, ran over and gave Ulysses an excited pat on his flank. Ulysses stepped backwards gingerly, and Jake noticed he was favouring his front left leg.

"You OK, boy?" he said in a concerned tone. He lifted up Ulysses's hoof and straight away, he saw what the problem was. A fragment of sharp glass from the crater had wedged itself under a loose iron horseshoe, and was digging into the sensitive hoof.

Carefully, so as not to shatter it, Jake worked the fragment backwards and forwards until it became loose.

"As soon as we make it to civilisation, you're getting yourself new horseshoes, my friend," said Jake, tossing the remains of the glassy fragment on the ground.

Ulysses let out a contented whinny and then, like a bolt of lightning, Jake suddenly realised exactly how to escape their predicament.

He raced over to the old farmhouse and started to clamber over the burnt wall. "Come on, Washington," he yelled urgently. "We've got ourselves work to do."

The soldiers aimed their rifles at the two motionless figures standing next to their single horse. Both had their hands raised high, but the captain of the troop column was wisely taking no chances.

"Don't move a muscle," he shouted. "Cover me, men," he ordered and urged his panting, sweaty cavalry horse forward.

Pistol drawn and cocked, the captain approached the figures, watching for any sudden moves. He kept the setting sun at his back, so the figures would be staring straight into the blinding afternoon light.

"This is Ute country," growled the captain suspiciously, when he drew near. "You like to explain what business you have out here?" He motioned to the figures to come closer, keeping his pistol trained upon them.

"We got robbed," pleaded the older of the two. "Those treacherous Utes robbed us of everything and left us with nothing but our horse."

Again, the captain sniffed suspiciously.

"Search them," he barked, keeping his weapon trained upon the strangers, while two soldiers dismounted and approached the pair cautiously.

A few seconds later, after a rough search, one of the soldiers saluted the captain.

"They ain't got nothing, Captain. No guns, nothing in their pockets, not even a saddlebag to hide anything in."

The captain eyed the two figures disdainfully. They clearly had nothing on them except the clothes on their backs. He wheeled his horse around, knowing he had better things to do than help fools who ventured into Ute country. He was impatient to reach the nugget of gold the Utes had informed him lay another day's ride to the east.

"Learn your lesson," snapped the captain. "Next time, you'll be lucky to get out of Ute country with either your horse or your lives."

The older of the two strangers tipped his hat respectfully and the younger copied the soldier in a salute.

"Fools," snorted the captain in derision, as he signalled the troop to form a column. With a shouted command, he kicked his heels forcefully into his horse's flank, and the soldiers thundered away in a cloud of yellow dust.

The two figures were left standing in the Utah sun. They watched the column of soldiers disappear across the landscape, and then they climbed back onto their horse.

"Come on, Ulysses," coaxed the older of the figures. "Only a couple more days, and I guarantee we'll get you some proper shoes."

Jake, Washington and Ulysses slowly headed off towards the setting sun.

8 A Family Secret

The greedy soldiers never found the fabled great gold nugget for which they'd paid the Utes handsomely. And the story of the Great Golden Nugget of Utah might have been forgotten, passed off as just another fanciful western campfire story – if it hadn't been passed down from generation to generation in two families, well respected in their communities.

"What happened to the great golden nugget?" asked the boy. "Was it really just a campfire story?"

"Oh, no," smiled his grandfather conspiratorially. "Those two characters and their trustworthy horse had a secret, you see. And, if you promise to keep the secret, I'll let you in on how they managed to get away with the great golden nugget of Utah."

The boy nodded eagerly. "I can keep a secret," he promised. "What did they do?"

Congressman Washington Freeman IV winked at his grandson, and pointed up at the family crest that hung on the wall.

"They just walked out with it – or should I say Ulysses did. See if you can guess how they managed that," he smiled.

"The Great Golden Nugget of Utah," said the boy, as he peered at the family crest. And slowly it dawned on him that the crest, which he'd seen on his grandfather's wall a hundred times, was really the final chapter of a story that was truer than he'd ever imagined.

"It is a true story," he gasped. "They made the gold into ..."

"Shh!" whispered his grandfather. "One day, you may be able to tell the story to your grandson. But until then, it's our secret, remember. Our family secret."

"Yes, sir!" said the boy emphatically.

Washington Freeman IV laughed. "It's been one hundred and fifty years since we called anyone "sir" in this household," he said. "Let's not start that habit again."